A Londoner by birth, Val Policella her husband and two children. She at an early age and still enjoys eating

Val has no training in cookery wh author of several books on food, and she does not contribute regularly to *The Gourmet* magazine, although she has written the odd shopping list. She is considered by many to be a first-class slob and her hobbies include pigging herself, and not washing up afterwards.

This is her first and last book as she says she won't be able to spare another two evenings to write a sequel. Val has two overriding ambitions – one, to be invited on to Desert Island Discs, and two, to get the tap fixed on the kitchen sink.

CARELESS COOKING

An Alternative Cookery Book

Val Policella

SPHERE BOOKS LIMITED

A SPHERE BOOK

First published in Great Britain by Sphere Books Ltd 1989

Reproduced, printed and bound in Great Britain by
Richard Clay Ltd, Bungay, Suffolk

ISBN 07474 04380

Sphere Books Ltd
A Division of
Macdonald & Co. (Publishers) Ltd
27 Wrights Lane W8 5TZ

A member of Maxwell Pergamon Publishing Corporation plc

A word of thanks: To my husband for his undying enthusiasm for anything other than this book. And to my sister for constantly lending me her support tights.

Contents

Introduction

First of all, who do I think I am? God knows. I've been going through an identity crisis since I was six. At least these days I know what I'm not. The list is endless but 'a good cook' is certainly on it somewhere. Is there any justification then in my having the audacity to write a cookery book? Well of course there isn't. So what? I'm doing it anyway and if you don't like it, tough titty.

Oh, you're still here are you? Okay then, let's get down to business. Hands up those of you who remember those June Whitfield adverts on the telly where she let her guests think their Birds Eye meal had been cooked by her own fair hand? What a sensible woman. The only difference between June and myself is that I can't be bothered trying to cover things up. I wasn't always like it – there was a time when I enjoyed the culinary art. And I was so *snotty* – everything had to be fresh, and if there was an unnecessarily complicated cooking method you could guarantee I'd use it. Then the children came along. A few years of 'Mummy, *you* be She-Ra' as I was doing the fish fingers, and elaborate entertaining slowly bit the dust. Frozen pastry and packet sauces became friends for life. As a result I'm now capable of preparing three courses for twelve people in fifteen minutes (and if you believe that, you must be sharing your brain with someone else and it's not your turn).

No, but really, all that *effort*. Can someone tell me what the point is of spending the whole day of your dinner party slaving over a hot gas hob if you wind up so tired you miss the bit in the conversation about Shirley Knott, the plumber and the leaky ballcock? And where were you when the wall-mounted boiler joke came up? Once upon a time you'd have shrieked sexism. Instead, gonzo-like, you stare at your caringly created Salmon en Croûte as it disappears into, oh yes, the most enthusiastic of gobs – ah but why do you have the feeling six quarter pounders with cheese would have been greeted with equal enthusiasm? Perhaps more if I was one of the guests.

Anyway, I digress. As you'd by now imagine, the recipes which follow break every rule in the (other) book(s), they certainly don't look up to much and they're probably pretty unhealthy to boot. However, if you approach them with a, shall we say, *relaxed* attitude, you may find one or two are almost edible. My basic approach to cooking is summed up in the title of this book, i.e. I couldn't care less. The fact remains though that stomachs need filling, and as your average dinner guest doesn't have the sensitive palate of Albert Roux why not prosper by a little cheating, in terms of time at least?

And as for presentation, well let's face it, viewing food as an art form's all very well but it's not such a pretty picture when it comes out the other end is it? I mean, would you flush a Picasso down the toilet? No, I thought not. Don't get me wrong, mind. I can enjoy a bit of expensive Nouvelle as much as the next person, particularly if the next person's paying for it. But if I were to try presenting three carrot strips and a bunch of juniper berries on a Saturday night chez moi, you can guarantee that whoever got the Peter Rabbit plate would soon cut me down to size. Ah well, such is life.

So, fellow cookaphobics, who knows, – perhaps 'Careless Cooking' will help free your own time in the kitchen somewhat so that you and your partner can enjoy the more pleasurable activities life has to offer. And after all, what better way to work up an appetite . . .

Note on Quantities

If you detect a hint of vagueness regarding the ingredient amounts, this is due to the fact that I've no idea how much food 'serves four' (or whatever). I always start off with at least three times more than any normal person would as I work on the principle of tasting everything several times as I go along. This is why I'm as fat as a pig.

Also, I like to make sure there's enough for seconds. Nothing worse than those dinner parties where you have to make sure you've got a secret Mars bar in your handbag for the journey home. Quantity, not quality, I always say.

Author's Note

Cookery writers are almost as bad as estate agents for trying to pull the wool over your eyes. Here are some of their favourite superlatives, redefined:

'delicate flavour'   tasteless
'exotic'   a bit daring for the in-laws
'this classic dish'   this old hat oh god not this
                         again dish
'aromatic'   can't get rid of the smell for
                         days
'rich and filling'   sickly
'family favourite'   the one they'll at least eat
'light lunch'   not enough
'satisfying lunch'   enough for some people but not me
'subtle blend of
   flavours'   boring

*

Starters

*

Jeeanti

Here's an unusual starter I picked up during my travels around Surrey.

Ingredients

Lots of ice
Lots of gin
Tablespoon tonic
Twist lemon
Couple corn chips

Method

Pour it out and knock it back.

NB Not suitable for a microwave.

Tomato Soup

Any recipe you'll find for tomato soup will have you spending three weeks getting the skins off. Fresh tomato soup is very nice but not worth all that palaver. Here's my way.

Ingredients

Lots of tomatoes
An onion or two
Sugar
Bit of basil
Stock

Method

Put everything in a blender and switch on. If you haven't got one, tough. Why are you still reading this? You can't possibly make it without one so go away and do some decorating or something. For the rest of you, I forgot to tell you to put the lid on first. If your kitchen now looks like there's been a massacre well never mind. It'll teach you to read the recipe through before starting. To continue, scrape the mixture off the walls, put in a pan and cook a while. Let it cool, then serve in glasses with vodka and Worcester sauce. There you are then. Bloody tomato soup.

Chickeno Mexicano

Personally I don't go a bundle on avocados so I'm hardly likely to tell you this is delicious, but the cat likes it and that's good enough for me. (He's always been his own person.) Use a young bird for this recipe. Ask the cashier at the supermarket for a copy of the death certificate. I'm sure she'll be happy to oblige.

Ingredients

Cooked chickeno
Avocado
Lemon juice
Olive oil
Small green chilli, finely choppedo
Small green pimento, ditto

Method

Sort of chop it up and mix together. Chill for a few hours. Arrange in a bowl as imaginatively as you can manage. Serve with a dish of rabbit Cat Treats.

Another reason I'm not keen on this one is the lack of alcohol. (I gather it's trendy not to drink these days, but then I still wear loons.)

Mushroom Toasts

I'd like to be able to tell you that the tastes and textures of these ingredients work particularly well together but I can't. I've only got the standard palate as opposed to the deluxe, but it tastes all right to me.

Ingredients

Mushrooms, sliced
Half a lemon
Fromage frais
Capers ⎫
Chives ⎭ chopped
Thick slices of wholemeal bread

Method

Cut rounds of buttered bread, put in oven, quite high, till crisp. Grate lemon rind finely and squeeze juice. Mix with other ingredients in a pan and gently heat through. Plonk a good spoonful onto each 'toast'. Serve immediately. Go on, hurry up.

A Real Pea Souper

When you're walking home from the station on a cold November evening and you can't see two feet in front of you because of the fog, the thought of this delicious soup won't help one bit as it's served cold.

Ingredients

Large packet frozen peas
Spring onions, chopped
14oz natural yoghurt
Lemon juice
Mint

Method

Cook peas and leave in water. Mix yoghurt, lemon, onions and mint. Add peas and water to rest. Season. Chill for at least an hour.

Come to think of it, November's just as good a time as any to have this. After all, the middle of July's not so blinking hot is it?

It's 8.00 pm. They're due at half past. You're up to your elbows in flour. There's lumps of pastry all over the floor. Your other half's enjoying a relaxing bath. You casually wipe sour cream through your hair. You put the finishing touches to the pie and accidentally poke a hole in it. You hear the plug being let out upstairs. You shout up that you want the water run again. You look in the cupboard for the pre-dinner nibbles. You've forgotten to buy them. You tread in the cat's bowl. You run upstairs and get undressed. You haven't even thought about a starter. You jump in the bath with your watch on. It's freezing. You let out a yell.

'Quick Chilli Dip – that's it!'

Ingredients

Mayonnaise
Chilli powder
Turmeric
Chopped chives (opshnul)
Grated onion
Tarragon vinegar

Method

You mix it all together. You taste it. Something's gone right. You look around for bits to dip in it. There's nothing. You start to cry. The doorbell rings. You fix your smile. You have a splendid evening.

Savoury Scramble

More like a mini-snackette than a starter but I'm not starting up a whole new section for one recipe.

Ingredients

Streaky bacon, chopped
Onion, chopped
Cooking apple, chopped
What no eggs?

Method

Come on now, chop chop. Put some butter in a pan and add ingredients. Fry. Serve on a bed. Oh sorry, of shredded raw spinach.

Alternatively, you can use this mixture to top a muffin or two. To do this, cram your muffins in the toaster till they start smoking. Put some gunk on top of each one and finish off with grated cheese. Place under grill. (Don't be tempted to put them back in the toaster. They don't fit – I know, I've tried.)

Japaneasy Fish

This is exquisite. And yet so simple. (Bit like me really.) If you've got the kind of drongoes to dinner who never veer far from a Nice Mixed Grill, this is the one to give them.

Ingredients

Any white fish fillets – cod'll do, plaice, trout, etc.
1 or 2 lemons
Ginger
Horseradish sauce
Cucumber

Method

Get skin off fish as best you can. Squeeze lemon juice and mix with horseradish and ginger to taste. Marinate fish overnight. Plonk on individual plates. Now take your cucumber, stare at it and try and invent an artistic garnish. Oh and don't wait until after they've eaten it to tell them the fish is raw. Do it as the forks enter the mouths – much more fun.

Crudités

As your guests settle in with their pre-nosh drinks, a few crudités passed around are always enjoyable:

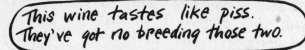

Les Escargots Reprievés

I was curious about cooking snails once so I looked up a recipe, as you do. It said to put them in a bowl covered with wire netting, stick them on a shady balcony and feed them on bran for a fortnight, after which I should cover them in salt, give them a shake and wait for them to froth. At the point where I was to 'pour off the slime' I gave it up as a bad job. I suggest you do the same.

*

Ontrays

*

Angelo's Tagliatelle

We first came across this dish in a restaurant in Florence*
where the proprietor, Angelo, was often to be seen vigor-
ously tossing his noodles.

Ingredients

Tagliatelle
Chicken livers, cut into small chunks
Double cream
Marsala

Method

Coat chicken livers in flour and fry in butter for a bit. Add
Marsala (about $\frac{1}{3}$ cup) and cook till reduced slightly.
Meanwhile put tag on to boil. Add cream to livers and
heat through gently. Pour over tagliatelle. NOT IN THE
SAUCEP – Oh dear. You really don't know much about
cooking, do you? I suppose I should have stated the
obvious. Ah well. I expect you're good at other things.
Brushing your hair perhaps, something like that?

---

* Printer's error: should read 'Hounslow'.

The Stuff of Loaf

You can serve this one hot at home, or cold on a picnic if you've forgotten to put the cooker in the boot. I wouldn't do it for a dinner party if I were you.

Ingredients

Uncut loaf
Pretty much anything as long as it won't go too soggy. Use your initiative
Cheese

Method

Cut the top off your loaf and keep it somewhere safe away from birds, etc. Pull out the bread inside. Crumb it and mix with whatever else you've got. Bung it all back in. Put a load of grated cheese on top. (This is to make the 'lid' glue back on but it doesn't always work.) Wrap it in foil. Put in the oven for a bit, not too high or it comes out like concrete. Let it cool for a while before slicing. A bloody mess but quite tasty.

Coley Thermidor

If coley is unavailable lobster makes a reasonable substitute.

Ingredients

Coley, Parmesan, Breadcrumbs

For the Not Proper Mornay Sauce:
Packet white sauce
Parmesan again
Cayenne

For the winey bit:
White wine
Onion
Dijon mustard (see that, I know some French)
No parmesan

Method

Push a sharp knife through the nerve centre of the coley if it's not dead yet. I wouldn't bother if it already is. Cut off the bits you can't eat and take out dem bones. Grill what's left in a lobster-shell shaped dish. Oh, don't you have one? Good Lord. Well never mind, carry on. Make up the Not Proper Mornay Sauce. In another pan (it won't kill you to wash up one more pan) fry the chopped onion gently in butter. Don't poke at it like that. Add a bit of white wine – go on, and a bit more – and some mustard. Boil fast until there's not so much of it and add to the sauce. Pour it on the coley. Sprinkle with breadcrumbs and parmesan and grill for a while longer. Serve with oven chips. (I do my own, but if I've got guests I pretend they're McCains, which says a lot about my chips.) (And my guests.)

A nice bottle of Asti Spumante served at room temperature would go well with this dish.

Farmhouse Hotpot

When Seth and Amos come in hungry after a mornin's ploughin' an' milkin', give 'em a treat.

Ingredients

Sausagemeat
Herbs
Cooking apple
Grated cheddar
Potatoes, peeled and sliced

Method

Line bottom of ovenproof dish with sausagemeat. Add herbs, then slices of apple, cheese and finally potato slices. Dab with butter. Bake for an hour or so, middly temp, until brown. And if anyone says, 'But I only wanted some houmous and raw veg,' stick one on them.

Goulash-ish

There's nothing like a really good goulash, and this is nothing like a really good goulash. But it'll do.

Ingreedyents

You don't have to use beef. If you've only got pork in the freezer let them eat pork. No-one's going to put you in detention. I don't think.
Where was I?
Oh yes, Onions
Garlic
Caraway seeds
Paprika
Tin crushed tomatoes
Stock } *adjust amounts to suit meat quantity*
tity
Sour cream

Method

Fry onion, garlic, caraway and pap for a bit in oil. Add a spot of flour, then toms, then a little stock but don't make it too runny. Bung your meat in a casserole dish, add sauce and stir things up. Cook slowly for a good long while and add sour cream at last minute. Serve with a noodle or two. And perhaps a salad. And perhaps a chunk of bread. And perhaps – oh dear, there I go again. Time for my elevenses. And then I must go to bed.

Steak and Kidney Pudding

I like this one because you can give your feet a good soak at the same time. After a hard day's shopping for cookware items in Habitat, you'll be thanking me for this little tip.

Ingredients

Tin of steak and kidney pudding

Method

Pierce tin and stand in boiling water for 45 minutes.

(The old ones are the best.)

Brains in Batter

A clever little supper dish.

Ingredients

Calves brains
Flour
Fritter batter

Method

Soak the brains in warm water for half an hour. (This is called brainwashing.) Remove skin, membranes and all the red thread. Blanch for 15 minutes in lemon juice and water. If they're still too slippery to hold put in freezer for ten minutes. In the meantime, go to the toilet and throw up. On your return, warn your loved one before he goes to put ice in his drink. If you feel like carrying on (this is called brainless) slice them into quarters, dry, coat with flour and batter, and fry in oil. Just before serving, phone

the pizza place so that you'll have an alternative if necessary. This is called a brainwave.

Bubble & Squeak II

Here's a handy one if you've got one of those expensive mixer affairs with attachments. My mum bought me one last Christmas so I'm a lucky bugger. You can use an ordinary grater as long as you've got some plasters ready.

Ingredients

Any grateable vegetable more or less
Any grateable meat/fish (I can't think of any, can you?)
Anything else grateable you fancy

Method

Put the grater attachment on the mixer. Put the stuff in. Press the button. Empty contents into dish. Dot with butter or pour a packet sauce all over it. Put a lid on it if you don't like it burnt. Stick it in the oven for a bit. That's it. Grate. Actually it's pretty revolting, isn't it? I nearly didn't put that one in.

I just can't decide about this one.

Maisonette Pie

This is my own version of the more traditional cottage pie. I've been making it on and off since the early days in our first flat.

Ingredients

Mince, onions, gravy, etc
Parsnips
Cream

Method

I'm particularly partial to parsnips. Well-mashed, lots of black pepper and cream, piled high and browned to a crisp. What more could a person want? (Well, I could do with a decent typewriter for a kick-off. And I'm desperate for a new winter coat. And boots. Of course we're well overdue for a holiday. But then the kids' room needs a new carpet. And the garden shed's knackered. So's the Hoover. And if the telly keeps going on the blink that'll be another thing. And Jack's outgrowing his bike and his shoes, and t'other one's buggy's on the verge of collapse. And then there's the *car*. Still. I've food in my stomach and that's the main thing.)

Grandma Policella's Baps

This next recipe has been in my family for years. I recently came across an exact imitation in a local fast-food outlet, and I have to admit it came a close second.

Ingredients

2 all-beef patties, special sauce, lettuce, cheese, pickles, all in a sesame seed bun

Method

Cook the patties on a very large griddle, put them in the bun with the other bits and place in a brightly-coloured box. Serve with almost cold fried potato sticks and the strangest apple pie I've ever seen.

Pasta, Spinach, Bacon and Cream Dish

I have to admit I pinched this one from another book but it's such a doddle it had to go in. I renamed it to protect the cook.

Ingredients

Pasta
Spinach
Bacon
Cream

Method

Obvious really. Cook the pasta. Chop up bacon and fry to a frazzle. Cut up the raw spinach. Stick it all in with the drained pasta and the cream and heat for a sec. Bit of parmesan and there you have it. Scrummo. In fact I think I'll go and make some right now, bye . . .

Poached Chops

This is one I discovered after having joined the local babysitting circle. You can adapt the basic principle to suit whatever's available at the time.

Ingredients

The half an onion that's stinking out the fridge
Tomorrow's lamb chops
The dead cabbage in the veg rack
The dregs of the week-old tin of tomatoes

Method

Cut off the mouldy leaves from the cabbage and try and squash them into the unemptied bin. Chop and fry the rest with the onion. Add the chops and later on the tomatoes. Squidge it round a bit from time to time. Woof it down quick before they get back. Don't answer the phone the next day.

Pancake Bake

When I discovered ready-made pancakes in a shop near me I bought up their entire stock. Everyone thinks you're brilliant when you do them so here's your chance to excel, although you'll have to take a bus to Hampton Hill to get them and they only sell them on Shrove Tuesday. I suppose you *could* make your own but sod that for a game of soldiers.

Ingredients

Quite a few pancakes
Tons of bolognaise
Yoghurt and sour cream mixed
Parmesan

Method

Cook your bolognaise and layer between pancakes, ending with bol. Cover liberally with yoghurt and sour cream and sprinkle with parmesan. Put in oven. Cut in wedges and serve with the Green, Red and Purple Salad on page 68. Actually, I take that back. Serve it with anything you like. Who am I to tell you what to do anyway? You can eat your own bogies with it for all I care.

Plummy Beef

Hairz a naice dish.

Buy a joint of best biff from Herrods. Put it in the huvven to cook. In a pan make a roux with flar and buttah. Mesh some tinned plums and edd to pan with a bittuv Shetto-nerf-du-Pep. Edd a sprinkle of sinmun. Mix till smooth. Pour over biff.

Ap-slootleh fairstrait, hizzen tit?

Actually, my old man loves this. But then he's no judge. His favourite meal of all time's mince, mash and processed peas. I only married him because I felt sorry for him. He's had a cruel life you know. It all started when he was about 12 – his school was holding a Parents' Day and they needed a first-year boy to top the human pyramid display. Naturally he volunteered (?) and naturally he fell off and broke his arm. A handful of concerned teachers gathered round him making sympathetic noises, until the ambulance arrived by driving straight across the 1st XI cricket square and that was it. His name was mud, not to mention his shorts.

Then there was the time he was helping his dad to change a wheel on the car and the jack shot off and went through his top lip.

And then even just a few years back there was the night when he was on stage (he's a musician – or near as damn it), posing on top of a monitor speaker, and he fell headlong into the orchestra pit.

There's not a day goes by that I don't appreciate the fact that I'm his wife.

Steak Tartare

I invited some friends round for dinner recently and they looked a little alarmed when I told them what we'd be eating. I didn't understand why but assumed they weren't great fish fans. See what you think anyway.

Ingredients

Birds Eye Cod Steaks
Tartare sauce

Method

Cook the steaks according to directions. That's easy enough isn't it? Even for someone like you. Now put a blob of sauce beside each. Yes of *course* on a plate. Jesus, who'd have this job?

This dish could be served with new potatoes and peas. I was cross with my guests for being so pathetic and didn't do them any veg so they *had* to eat the fish or it would notice too much. They managed to force it down and the evening went quite well after that.

NB I was a bit edgy when I wrote this. PMT probably.

35

Tweed Kettle

This traditional dish calls for the use of left-over cooked salmon. Of course, fresh salmon is so wonderfully cheap you're really likely to have plenty left over, aren't you? Still, you're probably quite rich if you can afford to fritter your money on little extras like cookery books.

Ingredients

New potatoes, scrubbed, cooked and cubed
Spring onions, chopped
Salmon, as above, cubed
Cayenne

Method

Soften onions in some butter. Add salmon and potatoes. You'll need more butter. Fry gently to avoid breaking up until browned.

Come to think of it, we've never once had leftovers in our house. Nothing makes it as far as the fridge with me around.

37

Piquant Lamb

Lamb with a pungent tangy sauce (sometimes also known as Sheep Dip).

Ingredients

Leg of lamb
Gravy
Tarragon vinegar
Capers
Mixed herbs
Tomato purée

Method

Roast lamb till nicely pink (I can roast in sunny Spain for a fortnight and still only be nicely pink). Make up gravy the way you like it. Add rest of ingredients until it tastes reasonable then chuck into a jug or something and serve alongside sliced meat.

What? Yes, yes, I heard you the first time, what do you mean 'Yukko Yukko'? I suppose you'd have preferred it as just gravy would you? Well perhaps you ought to be reading Phyllis Tyne's *Recipes for Morons* instead of this. I dunno, you try and broaden people's horizons and what d'you get? A load of jip. I'll give you blinking yukko, mate. This is a high class dish, which is more than can be said for you. Plebbo. Go and piquant someone else.

NB The amount of corn in this recipe may need to be adjusted to suit your taste.

Bacon and Cauliflower Cheese uh Flan

I invented this myself one day when I was supposed to be doing a caulicheese but I only had a little cauli so I thought I'd bung in some bacon to make it more filling but then I realised I didn't have any so I quickly thought on my feet and by using the pastry that I was going to use to make an apple pie came up with a flan instead and we had baked apples for pud. It was a difficult day but I got through it.

Ingredients

Frozen shortcrust
Cauli, cut up
2 eggs
$\frac{1}{3}$ pint milk and single cream mixed
Grated Red Leicester
Cayenne

Method

Make a flan base with pastry (you may find it easier to roll out once it's thawed). Cook cauli for five mins. Beat eggs and milk etc together. Drain cauli and put in flan case. Pour eggy stuff over and cover liberally with cheese. Stick in the oven till brown and solid. (Perhaps I should have chosen my words better there. Still, too late now.)

Spaghetti alla Puttanesca

Good basic stuff, this. Roughly translated, it means 'as a tart would cook it'. And before you smirk like that, remember it applies just as much to you if and when you choose to make it.

Ingredients

Spaghetti
Peppers – red, yellow, orange, green
Black olives
3 cloves of garlic, chopped
Parmesan

Method

Cut peppers into strips. Fry in olive oil for a while then add garlic and olives and cook for a bit more. Meanwhile get the spag on. When it's ready mix it all up (add a bit of fresh olive oil if necessary) and throw some parmesan at it. Oh sorry, I've got to go. One of my regulars has just arrived.

Vegetarian Supper

Poor old veggies, they come in for some stick. I heard a tale about a woman travelling on a plane, who when presented with a meaty meal announced she was vegetarian and asked if she could have something else. The stewardess went away and came back with a copy of the *Guardian*.

Ingredients

Haricot beans, cooked as per packet
Onions ⎫
Carrots ⎬ Fried till edible
Parsnips ⎭
Packet white sauce
Mashed potato
Cheese

Method

Mix up first four ingredients with the white sauce and put in casserole. Top with potato and grated cheese. Cook till brown.

The tricky thing I find with vegetarian stuff is what to serve it with.

Braised Beef with Basil

This is a difficult one if you don't know anyone called Basil, but see what you can do.

Ingredients

Braising steak
Onions
Tin tomatoes
Cornflour

Bas – Oh, I *see*. Sorry. Bit of a slip-up there. And now of course it's obvious I just steal all my recipes from other books. Well there you go. I never promised you a rose garden. Along with the sunshine there has to be a little rain sometimes. If you take you've got to give so live and let live or let go oh oh oh oh, I beg your pardon, I never promised you a – Oh God, sorry. I get so bored doing this. I never wanted to be a cookery writer you know. My real ambition is to be a country and western singer with big bosoms and a blonde wig, but I gather it's been done already. Still, life goes on and so does this recipe. Blend the cornflour with a bit of water and add to the other ingredients in a casserole. Cover and cook in a slow oven for $1\frac{1}{2}$ hours. Just time in fact for me to play you a little song I've just written. Perhaps you'd like to join in. Ready everybody? One, two, three:

What d'you think?

Caribbean Kid Stew

You should be able to find these ingredients at your local Wavy Line Shop, particularly if you live in a sleepy village in North Wales.

Ingredients

3lb kid
½lb cassava root
½lb cush-cush yams
½lb West Indian pumpkin
1 green plantain
6 corns of Melegueta pepper
1 chayote
1 green papaya
1 tablespoon tamarind pulp
2 tablespoons molasses
Fresh coconut milk
Peanut oil
Frozen peas

Method

What, you mean you got hold of that lot? Oh, except the peas, I see. Well they are vital to the success of the dish I'm afraid, so it looks like it's no go.

(Phew, that was close. Fancy anyone thinking it was a serious recipe, I only put it in for a giggle. That'll teach me.)

Turkey Cobbler

Boxing Day. Cold turkey and lots of it. What to do, eh? Every year the same tough decision. Well try this. If you like.

Ingredients

Leftover dried-up turkey
Chicken Chasseur packet mix
Packet scone dough

Method

Make up sauce and mix with turkey in an oven dish. Make up scone dough and roll out to $\frac{1}{2}''$ thick. Using a smallish round pastry cutter, make circles and put on top of gunk. Bake till cooked through and golden.

And that's what you do with your load of old gobblers.

Poulet aux Trente Gousses d'Ail
(Chicken cooked with thirty cloves of garlic)

Well. Who's going to take a chance on this one then? My husband plays in a rock band and we always have this for lunch on the day of a gig. That way, if he's ever tempted to stray into the arms of a passing groupie I can be sure the encounter will be over before it's begun – unless she's got halitosis herself of course in which case he's welcome to her.

Ingredients

Chicken pieces
Trente gousses d'ail
Herbs
Olive oil
Brandy

Method

The trick of course is to keep the garlic cloves whole. Place them with the airbs in the bottom of a cocotte.* Sprinkle with oil. Put chicken on top. Cover, cook on low heat for two hours. Add water if nec. When the time's up, remove cocotte from the heat – I'm sure he'll be relieved. Pour the brandy over and light with a match. Cover with lid while still flaming. Leave for a few mins then serve. Strain sauce and pour on top.

Last time I cooked this a few of the chaps from Twicken-ham Fire Brigade popped in to join us but unfortunately it had all gone.

* See glossary. *Now*, or you won't get the joke.

An Indian Feast

Serious stuff now chaps. These are a few totally unauthentic Indianish dishes which I've inflicted on several groups of friends. They take very little time to prepare compared to doing it the proper way, and as long as you don't invite Madhur Jaffrey you'll probably get away with it.

Choose any or all of the following:

Tin Chicken Korma sauce	*Follow instructions on tin.*
Chicken	*Add nuts towards end.*
Cashews, quite a lot	*Sprinkle shredded coconut on top.*
Spinach	*Melt some butter. Add half*
Packet Biriani mix	*the packet contents and then chopped spinach.*
Cauliflower	*Melt some butter. Add a*
Ginger	*load of ground ginger and a cauli chopped up small.*

46

Pakoras	*You can buy these ready made and just heat them up in the oven.*
Naan	*As above. (You can get it in Waitrose.)*
Mint Raita	*Shove a spoonful of mint sauce in some yoghurt and chill.*
Basmati rice	*Don't forget to add oil to the water and a pinch of turmeric.*
Papadums	*Buy the ones you can grill but don't take your eyes off them.*
Orange and Onion Salad	*Cut up some oranges and spring onions and mix together.*

Lime pickle if you know anyone who can eat the stuff

And don't forget the amber nectar.

Ode to Food

When I first approached Sphere with my manuscript they said I was in with a chance but that I'd have to come up with more recipes as there weren't enough. I'd done six, but these people want blood, I tell you. Anyway, I've been up for three weeks solid now cooking and I must say I'm getting a little sick of it. So to break the monotony and yet still give You The Reader the value for money you so graspingly demand, I've added yet another string to my bow and become a food rapper. Here's the result – take it or leave it:

Me, I love food. Don't care if it's a biscuit
bubble'n'squeak, or a nice
bit of brisket.
À la carte, à la pub, dinner
brunch, high tea,
looking for grub, that's where
you'll find me.
Half a dozen oysters,
A ham and pickle roll.
And I'll never say no to
a good spag bol—

I can stack away a cassoulet,
a cauli and a cake,
and I'll still find room for a
triple shake.
I'm a sucker for sweets. I can
always say cheese.
I've been known to get passionate
on processed peas.
It's a funny old world for
a girl like me—

If you want to look a cracker then you're not allowed to eat.
But I'll never be a thin thing, I'm never so vain.
I was on a diet once but, I couldn't take the strain.
So I'll give up ever thinking I'll be lithe and lean,
and I'll aim to be the first British Sumo Queen.
If your times eaten up with calorie count,
then you're last years bore, not a shadow of doubt.
There's a lesson I've learnt and it's one I want to preach,
If you're HALF a 'Real Woman', then you've
          got to eat quiche . . . . .

And chips, And pizzas,
      And onion bhajis,
And tutti fruitti
pudding with orange
    foam sauce,
And . . . . .

*

Veg

*

Potatoes

A much underutilized vegetable, the potato, but one which I think we'll be seeing more and more of in the shops. This is a trendy way of doing them that I got off my friend Jill who lives in Beckenham.

Ingredients

One potato, two potato,
three potato, four (whatever you need really)

Method

Cut the potatoes as if slicing them but don't cut right through. (No, you don't peel them first, I'd have said so if I'd wanted you to peel them. Stop butting in.) Dot with butter, wrap in foil, put them in the oven and ignore them for a good while. Theoretically they should open out and look very pretty but I wouldn't bank on it.

An alternative to this recipe but still using this versatile vegetable is POTATO PURÉE. Just boil up some potatoes and mash them. This will be sure to impress your guests.

Pois Surgelés

By omitting the lettuce, spring onions and sour cream, this is a handy 'store cupboard' recipe for those unexpected dinner guests, as long as they're not very hungry.

Ingredients

Packet frozen peas
Decent lettuce
Spring onions
Sour cream

Method

Oh God, do I have to lead you by the hand every bloody time? Can't you work it out for yourself just once in your life?

Carrot Cake

I've always been a little confused that this has appeared in the Desserts section in cookery books when it's so obviously a vegetable.

Ingredients

Carrots
Oh, hundreds of other things

Method

I've lost interest in this one. Look it up in a proper book.

Stir-flied Wegetables

A wok cooks evenly and quickly and its shape concentrates the heat on the food. However, an old chipped enamel saucepan with no handle and rusty lumps at the bottom will do the job almost as well.

Ingredients

Bean sprouts (Yes, I hate them too but one feels one mustn't be too subjective)
Cabbage
Carrots
Green beans
Celery
Onion
Garlic
Ginger
Lemon
Soya sauce

Method

Cut up the veg just like you see in pictures of woks, and shove everything in with a bit of veg oil. Stir, fry, whatever you feel like really. Add some tahini if you have some, and if you have some, could you please write and tell me what it is? I looked it up in the dictionary but the nearest definition I could find was 'a crushing-mill for ores worked by horse-power', and that didn't sound quite right, I thought.

Creamed Watercress

This is a good accompaniment for bland roast meats or boring fish, neither of which sound worth cooking in the first place.

Ingredients

Loads of watercress, at least 8 bunches
Hefty lump of butter
Double cream

Method

Cut off coarse stalks. Cook rest in salted boiling water for 5

mins max. Drain. Squeeze out moisture. Put hands under cold tap to relieve burning. If this doesn't work, put hands under cold tap having first turned it on. Melt butter gently, add watercress, simmer for 10 mins, stirring occasionally. Add cream and lots of black pepper. Heat through gently.

And if you eat this regularly you'll avoid getting scurvy. Which is useful to know, isn't it?

Beetroot Soufflé

If you tell people what this is first I doubt whether anybody'll want to eat it. On the other hand, if you don't tell them, the colour may lead their imaginations astray and they'll say no anyway. You can always eat it all yourself. That's probably what I would do.

Ingredients

1 lb cooked beetroots, skinned
Mustard
6 fl oz orange juice
4 eggs
3 tblspns crnflr

Method

Liquidize beetroot, mustard and half the juice. Mix crnflr
with rest of juice, heat until it thickens. Add to liquidizer
and press again. Separate eggs, and add yolks to mixture
one at a time. Whisk the whites until stiff and fold in. Put
in a soufflé dish and cook fairly high for 20 mins at least
till risen and soufflé-ish.

Mmmm, that was delicious.

Ratatouille sans Aubergine, Courgette, Poivron et Ail, mais avec Concombre instead

(Two recipes in one – saves me doing one for ratatouille.)

Ingredients

3 cucumbers, peeled and cut lengthwise
Olive oil
Onion, chopped
1 lb tomatoes, chopped
Cumin

Method

Scrape seeds out and cut cukes into bite size pieces (in my case this would mean leaving them whole). Heat oil in pan and get onion going, add tomatoes, cumin and pinch of sugar. Put in cucumbers, cover and simmer for about half an hour. Serve with a bowl of sour cream. If I had my way, I'd serve everything with a bowl of sour cream as it's my most scrummy yummy favourite thing in the world, next to Tom Berenger. (I'd give anything to get next to Tom Berenger. Perhaps if I sent him a copy of this book he'd be so impressed he'd fly straight over to meet me. Yes, yes, I'm sure that's the answer. I'll get on to it.)

Cabbage in Mint sauce

Am I the only person in the world who likes cabbage? I used to eat everybody's at school and still go back for seconds.

Ingredients

Cabbage, shredded
Packet white sauce
Mint
White wine vinegar

Method

Boil cabbage for a couple of mins. Make up sauce. Add mint and simmer for a bit. Stir in vinegar and seasoning to taste. Pour over cabbage. Hang on, what's that big green lump? Oh for heavens sake, you don't put a whole clump of mint in, you idiot. Well, yes, I know I didn't tell you otherwise. I suppose it's all my fault, is it? Okay then. Anything else while you're at it? Oh, I *see*. Well, thank you very much. That's what I get for all my trouble, is it? 'You're fat.' Well you've got a big nose and tree trunk legs and you can't cook to save your life. What do you say to that then? Where are you going, I haven't finished yet. AT LEAST I COULD DIET IF I WANTED TO – YOU CAN'T CHANGE YOUR LEGS CAN YOU? Anyway, I like being fat. I must do, I was nearly a feminist once. Oh bloody Nora. Who's going to eat all this cabbage? Ah well . . .

Nutty Kale

I can't think of anything funny to say about this one.

Ingredients

Kale – plenty of it as it boils away to nothing
Toasted almonds
Chicken Oxo

Method

Trim off stems from kale and remove hard ribs from leaves. Chop up and cook in chicken stock for a bit. Drain. Add nuts.

I still can't think of anything. Well, all right, everyone's entitled to an off day now and then. I don't suppose Lenny Henry can keep it up all the time either. He can? Wow.

Hang on a minute, how do *you* know?

*

Salads

*

652 Bean Salad

You've probably seen the odd recipe for 'Three Bean Salad'. I've always thought this was a bit on the stingy side, so here's my version.

Ingredients

652 black-eyed beans
Spring onions
Bottled Italian dressing

Method

Soak the beans for 12 hours. (That should get those dirty marks out.) Boil in fresh water for 10 minutes, then cover and cook for half an hour. Drain and mix with spring onions and dressing. This doesn't really go well with anything as the Italians put so much garlic in their dressing it's all you'll be able to taste, but then that's probably just as well because black-eyed beans are probably the most boring things a person could eat. They have got one thing going for them though . . . they help you go pooz.

Stop STARING at me like that. I'M ONLY drowning you.

Green Salad

What better sight on a warm summer's day than a bowl of crisp green salad on that nice white patio table you got cheap from the petrol station?

Ingredients

Watercress*
That curly stuff, what is it? Endive*
Chicory*
Some sort of dressing (try Elastoplast)

Method

Toss. Serve with practically anything. Most people will say yes to a nice bit on the side.

   *Optional. (Some people don't like watercress, endive or chicory, so as an alternative try using limp lettuce, whole tomatoes and beetroot cubes, but of course you won't be able to call it 'Green Salad' then.)

Broccoli and Blue Cheese Salad

You'd better prepare this quite soon after buying the ingredients or your kitchen will begin to smell quite charming.

Ingredients

Broccoli, I'm afraid it's got to be fresh really
Nuts, any old mixture
Cabbage ⎫
Onion ⎬ *smallish amounts, chopped finely*
Carrots ⎭
Bit of Stilton, crumbled
Olive oil
Red wine vinegar
½ teaspoon chilli powder

Method

Cut up broccoli a bit. Make up dressing. Put everything together and mix.

Well, that should get the old sluices open.

Salade de Tomates

I knew a little boy once who had a fear of tomatoes. I didn't like them much myself when I was young but I can't say I was ever *afraid* of them. Onions yes, but not tomatoes.

Ingredients

Lots of those little baby tomatoes that cost an absolute fortune
Several basil leaves, chopped
French dressing

Method

Mix basil with dressing and chuck over toms.

I know what you're thinking. This is the dullest recipe in the whole book. So what? Mind your own business. I don't suppose you're in the middle of writing a bestseller, are you? No, I thought not. Far easier to sit there and criticize mine, isn't it? Pardon? What do you mean, it's your job? What, someone *pays* you to be thoroughly objectionable? Sounds the ideal career for me, where do I sign?

Any Old Rubbish Salad

When I first started cooking (about three weeks ago), I took a few chances with mixing unusual ingredients and the results were very exciting. My 'Spaghetti Banana' and 'Trout with Fried Eggs' are now family favourites. Here's an interesting suggestion:

Ingredients

Whatever you like really
Your choice of dressing

Method

With this recipe I'm trying to get you to think for yourself. It's a bit of a gamble I'll grant you, but the results are bound to be good if you convince yourself you can do it. Well yes, *exactly*, Roger – I'm sure lettuce and tomato would work very well together. You *see*, Roger can do it and so can you. Off you go now.

Californian Salad

I hope there are no Californians reading this. It's just that Twickenham Salad didn't have the same ring.

Ingredients

Iceberg lettuce
Celery
Peaches
Apples
Pecan nuts
Orange juice
Olive oil
Tarragon

Method

Shred, dice, stone, slice, chop, squeeze, pour and pinch, as required.

Meat Salad

I once tried to convince my son that the salad I was urging him to eat was actually a new type of cheeseburger. Naturally it didn't work as he's not stupid, and I am. This is the nearest thing to salad that I can get him to eat although he doesn't like the watercress or olives.

Ingredients

Mortadella
Pastrami
and any other trendy sort of meat, thickly sliced
Cheese
Watercress
Olives
Mayonnaise with half a teaspoon chilli powder in it

Method

Cut meat into long strips, cheese also. Mix with mayo. Artistically arrange meat on a bed of watercress with olives on top (sounds like a Swedish blue film – even more so if it was Olaf's On Top).

*

Afters

*

Designer Pudding

Correct me if I'm wrong, but I think I've pipped Bibendum to the post with this one.

Ingredients

Bananas
Ice cream
Raspberry jam
Nuts

Method

Now you may be thinking this looks remarkably like a banana split from the ingredients and you're right. I'm sure you can figure out what to do. It's probably come back in fashion by the time this book's out, but if not just stick something peculiar on top, like a geranium cutting, and Bob's your uncle.

Fruit Kebabs

These speak for themselves, which is an added bonus at dinner parties if the conversation is running a little dry.

Ingredients

Fruit

Method

Take the fruit and stick it on skewers. You can peel it and cut it up first if you prefer. Dot with beurre and grill. Serve with rice, pitta bread and a nice green salad.

Chestnut Mousse

A touch precise for my liking this one, but a casual attitude with mousse could result in either a drink or a lump of breezeblock.

Ingredients

¾ pint can unsweetened chestnut purée
¾ pint whipped double cream
2 egg whites
grated rind of ½ orange
4oz brown sugar

Method

Mix everything together except the egg whites. Beat these until they're stiff and crying for mercy, and fold into other stuff. Chill for a few hours. Apply to hair and blow dry in usual style. What we'll do for fashion, eh?

Apple Jelly Mould

This is one of the few things I really enjoy making. It's the risk element. Some people jump from planes, others scuba dive, I turn out moulds.

Ingredients

Packet lemon jelly
Pint unsweetened apple purée
Sultanas
Chopped nuts

Method

Dissolve jelly in $\frac{1}{4}$ pint boiling water. Add apple and sultanas. Let it set slightly then add nuts. Rinse out your rabbit mould with water and pour stuff in. Chill till set. To turn out, loosen sides with knife, then dip rabbit in hot water for 30 secs (don't submerge him for God's sake). There. Exciting, wasn't it? Okay fishface, chacun à son goût.

Mince Pies

Everyone loves mince pies at Xmas. Well usually. I make batches of them for various members of my family and they all pretend they're delicious but there must be something not quite right as I've noticed one or two of them being used as doorstops. I wish they had the courage to tell me to my face that they don't want them, but instead we go through this ridiculous charade every bloody year. It's got to the stage now where I positively enjoy putting them through it. I don't know, I can't see where I'm going wrong. My puff pastry's as rough as anyone else's and I always use best quality lean mince, so they can't get me on that one. Little dollop of cream, delicious.

Still, I think I may call it a day this year. Unless anyone's got any tips?

Cholesterol Pud

Anyone who knows me will vouch for the fact that I'm capable of talking the hind legs off 33 donkeys and usually do. We still have one or two friends left who, for reasons best known to themselves, accept this situation and occasionally invite us to dinner. Well, a very strange thing happened on one such evening quite recently. The pudding served up was so divine it actually caused me to stop mid-flow. And when I tell you that what I'd been talking about was my junior school hearthrob, Billy Laing, who I'd married in a spectacular playground wedding despite the fact that he used to spend more time setting fire to his farts in front of his pals than he did with me, you can see it was pretty riveting stuff. If you're out there Bill, this is for you.

Ingredients

Pineapple chunks, tinned or otherwise
$\frac{2}{3}$ *double cream to $\frac{1}{3}$ Greek yoghurt*
Demerara

Method

(Make it the day before you need it.) Whisk cream till it's really really thick. Add to yoghurt. Drain pineapple. Add to rest. Mix. Cover with lots of sugar. Put in fridge.

I'd like to say thanks to Sue for the recipe but I was taught never to speak with my mouth full.

Le Brie Chaud

This one sounds posh, dunnit?

Ingredients

1 whole Brie
Almonds
Fruit

Method

Cut the rind off the top of the cheese. Cover it with toasted almonds. No, not the rind, the cheese. Put in a dish in the oven until it's a bit runny. You'll find this is more likely to happen if you turn the oven on. Serve with cut up bits of fruit to dip it in. Brielliant.

Slimmer's Pudding

There's actually no such thing, but I felt obliged to offer something up for those of you stupid enough to bother dieting.

Ingredients

Artificial sweetener
Water
Skimmed milk
Lemon juice
Cottage cheese
Curd cheese

Method

Well it certainly seems a winner with those ingredients, doesn't it?

Mix it all up thoroughly until it looks like it's been eaten once already. Come to think of it, why not just chuck it straight down the toilet now and cut out the middle man? Saves wear and tear on the old gut. Or even better, why not nip down to the deli and buy an enormous chunk of cheesecake instead? It's up to you, of course.

I wonder if the magazine *Slimming Weakly* would be interested in reproducing this recipe ... I'll send it to them now.

Apple Yorkshires

A right scrumeh treat. Poot thees ont ayble 'n thou'll hear nowtboot praise.

Ingredients

Jar of stewed apples
Frozen Yorkshire puddings – I know, wonderful, isn't it?
(Both Waitrose again. No, I don't work there but perhaps I should.)

Method

Cook Yorkshires as instructed. Warm up the apple and plonk a dollop in the centre of each one. Serve hot with cream. Roast beef – who needs it?

Bread and Butter Pudding

I have to admit 5.30 p.m. is not my best time of day. Coincidentally this is often when the children are tired, bad-tempered and generally revolting, but I don't suppose one has anything to do with the other. Anyway, the little poppets are entitled to some tea at this time and I do my best to provide such a service, even though I'd rather go to the pub. Here's a nice old-fashioned pudding which I'm sure you've come across at some time.

Ingredients

Bread
Butter
Strawberry Jam

Method

Butter two slices of bread. Spread one with jam. Put the other on top. Cut in half. Repeat process. Put cut halves on a plate. Sling it onto the table, say 'Now stick that in your gobs and shut up' and go and nurse your guilt in a quiet corner.

Crème Caramel

When I was younger I went with my family on holiday to Ibiza and stayed in the Galeon Hotel. Every evening they had a different pudding on the menu, sometimes it was Galeon Pudding, sometimes Cartago Pudding (the sister hotel down the road) and once or twice Chocolate Pudding. Whatever we ordered, we always got Crème Caramel. I have fond memories both of that holiday and of this dessert.

Ingredients

Rhubarb
Caster sugar
6 oz flour
4 oz butter
Demerara

Method

Cut up the rhubarb and give it a bit of a wash. Put in an oven dish with a decent amount of sugar, at least 2 oz. Make up the crumble topping by blending the flour with the cut-up butter using the tips of your fingers. Add about 4 oz demerara, mix and put on top of rhubarb. Bake for about half an hour.

Another thing I remember about the holiday was my sister wearing shoes with 4″ platforms down to the beach each day, and my mum refusing to walk with her. I think it was because she felt short next to her, although it could have been the fact that there were 99 stony steps and it used to take her the whole morning to walk down. We used to hear her coming for ages before she finally turned up.

Yummy Yummy Chocolate Cake

Does anyone remember those Cadbury competitions we used to do at school? You won a tin of Bourneville chocs if you wrote a good essay about the cocoa bean or something. I won hundreds of course. My dad keeps his screws in the tins even to this day.

Ingredients

4 oz plain chocolate
Good size blob of butter
1 egg
Half a packet of ginger biscuits
Smidge orange juice
Tin of pears, drained and cut up a bit

Method

Put choc in a bowl and melt over a pan of hot water. Personally I melt over Tom Berenger, but you just do what feels right. Get the butter going in another pan. Whisk egg until frothy. Add choc, melted butter, crushed bikkies, juice and pears to egg. (I expect you wish you'd started with a bigger bowl, don't you?) Put the mixture in a flan dish and press flat. Stick it in the fridge to set. Have a bath, put on your dressing gown, take the cake, a jug of cream and a spoon, plonk yourself on the settee, turn on *Dallas* and eat the whole thing straight from the dish.

*

Party Buffet

*

Party Buffet

I always think there's enough to do when you're getting a party ready, what with putting up the fairy lights and choosing which discs to play, without having to think about the food as well. So here are my suggestions for quick and easy buffet fare guaranteed to appeal:

Open Sandwiches:	*Take a thick white sliced loaf, butter each slice, spread with Marmite and cut in half.*
Mixed Seafood Platter:	*Empty some packets of Scampi Fries and Java Crackers into a dish.*
Cod Roe Dip:	*Open a tub of taramasalata. Serve with Ritz Crackers if you can still get them anywhere.*
Assiette de Charcouterie:	*Arrange slices of spam, chicken roll and haslet on a plate and garnish with a large pickled onion.*

Pizza Pissartist: *And we won't be inviting him again after last time.*

Humus: *This always goes down well at other people's parties, although it hasn't been so popular at my own. Perhaps I'm not going to the right garden centre.*

And of course the ones they leave behind – stale French bread and hard cheese. Delicious.

*

Special Dinner Party Menu for Six

*

Special Dinner Party Menu for Six

Here's my suggestion for a real Cordon Blurr dinner menu guaranteed to have your guests singing your praises from beginning to end . . .

PICKLED EGGS

*

SOUSED HERRINGS

*

JUGGED HARE
with
CANNED PEAS

*

STEWED APPLES

*

POTTED CHEESE

*

BLACK COFFEE
and
ALKA SELTZER*

* It's always a good idea to pop one or two into your glass of wine towards the end of the evening.

*

Cooking for Kids

*

Cooking for Kids

All the recipes in this book can be adapted to suit young children by the simple addition of one bottle of tomato ketchup per serving.

Glossary of Food and Cooking Terms

À la:	Be braised
À la carte:	Meals on wheels
Al Dente:	Biting food critic
Aloo Gobi:	Traditional Indian greeting
Antipasto:	Not very keen on lasagne
Baking blind:	Method used when contact lens has dropped in cake mix
Barbecue:	Long wait at the hairdresser's
Bierwurst:	Watney's
Bind:	Cooking
Bismarck Herring:	Fish dish which always goes down well
Boeuf Bourgignon:	French for Beefburger & Onion
Bombay Duck:	Confused fish
Brill Soufflé:	A really good soufflé
Brine:	A friend of ours
Brownies:	See 'Straining'
Canary Pudding:	Well I kept warning him to shut up . . .
Candied fruit:	Quentin Crisp
Capers:	Jolly japes
Chard:	Black pudding
Chestnuts:	*Sun* readers
Chicken:	Cowardly
Chicken Chaud-Froid:	In a real state
Chocolate-beater:	Slimmer of the Year
Chuck steak:	Well, the sell-by date's there for a reason
Clarified butter:	It's a sort of yellow spread you have on bread. *Now* do you understand?

Cock-a-leekie:	A wee Scottish soup
Cocotte:	Male nudist sunbather
Coq au Vin:	Bit of a plonker
Coquille:	Full of oneself
Couscous:	When used repeatedly, useful expression for calling the cat in
Crème fraîche:	Cream not at all fresh
Crèpe:	What one darz in the privseh of one's airn lairvtreh
Croquette:	Tubbs's partner
Danish Blue:	Emanuelle in Copenhagen
Darne:	Polite alternative for 'Shit, I've just sliced my finger off with the sodding bread knife'
Deep fat fryer:	Profound tubby clergyman
Defrosting the freezer:	What you have to do when you can't get the door shut
Diplomatic Pudding:	Tactful tart
Dips and Spreads:	Sounds like my bottom
Drawing game:	Noughts and crosses
Drop scones:	Result of mislaid oven mitt
Dusting:	No idea about this one, sorry
Eggplant:	In vitro fertilization
Floating Island:	Another record company going public?
Flounder:	Have a bit of trouble
Forcemeat balls:	This doesn't bear thinking about
Fowl:	Tapioca, semolina – that sort of thing
Freezing:	Bloody cold
Fritter:	Spend recklessly
Gooseberry fool:	Thick-skinned hanger-on

Gourmet:	Edie
Grease:	Motorway services fry-up
Grind:	Cooking
Grouse:	A good whinge
Hanging game birds:	Gosh, that's a bit severe, isn't it?
Haute Cuisine:	Posh name for porridge
Hash Browns:	Yeah, far out man . . .
Herb chopper:	Runaway lawnmower
Home-made wine:	Another name for brake fluid
Irish Coffee:	Coffee flavoured with Irish whiskey and topped with thick cream
Jacket potatoes:	Then he had some pudding
Joint:	See 'Hash Browns'
Ketchup:	What you have to do if you get a bit behind
King Prawn:	A real wally
Langue de Chat:	Cat got your tongue?
Laying the table:	Whatever turns you on
Mangetout:	Greedy pig
Meatball stew:	Balls to you and all
Microwave:	Useful appliance for heating up takeaways bought in bulk and frozen
Monkfish:	Creature of habit
Naval Orange:	Accompaniment for belly pork
Nouvelle Cuisine:	Stingy portions
Offal:	Not very good at all

Paris-Brest:	Pigalle-originated pastry
Pawpaw:	What I'll be if nobody buys this bookbook
Passion fruit:	Hot date
Pea Soup:	See 'Cock-a-leekie'
Pine Nuts:	Lovers of stripped furniture
Plaice with Oranges:	Greengrocer's
Popcorn:	The Sweet
Porridge:	One's morning oats
Pot-au-Feu:	Better call 999
Preparing and dressing a crab:	You have your hobbies, I have mine, okay?
Profiteroles:	Successful ear-piercing business
Prune:	See 'King Prawn'
Raising agents:	Cambridge speciality
Rub in:	Go on a bit
Salami:	Abbrev. for the Salvation Army
Sauerkraut:	Bitter German
Scrag end of neck of lamb:	Well, that sounds nice, doesn't it?
Shoo Fly Pie:	Soon see this one off
Slow cooker:	Not me
Smorgasbord:	Abbrv. for the South Melstone and Overhampton Regional Gas Board
Snow Eggs:	Better buy some then
Spare ribs:	Often found just above spare tyre
Sponge:	Scrounge
Spotted Dick:	Oh dear, oh dear
Steaming:	Furious
Straining:	Digestive disorder
Summer pudding:	Another name for ice cream
Swede:	Bjorn Borg

Trotters:	See 'Brownies'
Tripe:	Collective noun for most of the recipes herein
Victoria Sandwich:	British Rail snack
Vin Ordinaire:	Ford Transit
Waffle:	Rhubarb rhubarb rhubarb
Wok:	Candy stick found in places like Bwighton
Yorkshire pudding:	Very moorish

THE END

Index

FOOD FIT TO EAT

British Nutrition Foundation

Can we survive our diet and the people who control it?

If you want the facts about your food – to understand the basic nutrition, get more goodness into your food preparation, or just outsmart the neighbourhood muesli set – then *FOOD FIT TO EAT* is for you.

What is in our food, who puts it there and what does it do to us when we eat it?

Is processed food fit to eat, or the possible cause of allergies and chronic artery and intestinal illnesses leading to early death?

Are there secret agreements between food manufacturers and government to keep the public in ignorance about additives and ingredients?

A prominent toxicologist and nutritionist, a journalist and a former senior manager in the food industry combine in a searching and understandable look at the food we eat from production to consumption, and explain the processes it passes through, the role of additives and the effects on the human system of manufactured foods. They examine the relationship between the food industry and government and draw the line between fact and propaganda absent from so much contemporary food writing.

If you want to read the truth about the food industry . . . read *FOOD FIT TO EAT*.

0 7474 0314 7   REFERENCE   £3.99

STARK
BEN ELTON

Stark have more money than God and the social
conscience of a dog on a croquet lawn. What's more,
they know the Earth is dying.

Deep in Western Australia where the Aboriginals used
to milk the trees, a planet-sized plot takes shape. Some
green freaks pick up the scent. A Pommie poseur, a
brain-fried Vietnam Vet, Aboriginals who lost their land
. . . not much against a conspiracy that controls society.
But EcoAction isn't in society; it just lives in the same
place, along with the cockroaches.

If you're facing the richest and most disgusting
conspiracy in history, you have to do more than stick up
two fingers and say "peace".

0 7474 40390 2   GENERAL FICTION   £00.00

DEREK TANGYE

JEANNIE
A LOVE STORY

When Jeannie and Derek Tangye withdrew to a cliff-top
flower farm in Cornwall, sophisticated London society
protested, but an even wider circle was enriched by the
enchanted life which they shared and which Derek
recorded in the *Minack Chronicles*. Jeannie died in 1986,
and, in tribute to her extraordinary personality, her
husband has written this portrait of their marriage. The
delight of the *Minack Chronicles* is here – the daffodils,
the donkeys and the Cornish magic. And all the fizzle
and pop of champagne days at the Savoy is captured as
Jeannie dazzles admirers from Danny Kaye to Christian
Dior.

'All her life she belonged to the glitter, the drama, the
heroism and the sacrifice of her time. Jean and Derek
have taught a lot of people how to live'
John Le Carré

Don't miss the *Minack Chronicles* by Derek Tangye,
also available in Sphere Books

0 7474 0357 0   AUTOBIOGRAPHY   £2.99

All Sphere Books are available at your bookshop or newsagent, or can be ordered from the following address: Sphere Books, Cash Sales Department, P.O. Box 11, Falmouth, Cornwall TR10 9EN.

Please send cheque or postal order (no currency), and allow 60p for postage and packing for the first book plus 25p for the second book and 15p for each additional book ordered up to a maximum charge of £1.90 in U.K.

B.F.P.O. customers please allow 60p for the first book, 25p for the second book plus 15p per copy for the next 7 books, thereafter 9p per book.

Overseas customers, including Eire, please allow £1.25 for postage and packing for the first book, 75p for the second book and 28p for each subsequent title ordered.